The Best Selection

of Nepal Recipes

Middle-Eastern Dishes Made Simple for Everyone

BY: Valeria Ray

License Notes

A Special Reward for Purchasing My Book!

Thank you, cherished reader, for purchasing my book and taking the time to read it. As a special reward for your decision, I would like to offer a gift of free and discounted books directly to your inbox. All you need to do is fill in the box below with your email address and name to start getting amazing offers in the comfort of your own home. You will never miss an offer because a reminder will be sent to you. Never miss a deal and get great deals without having to leave the house! Subscribe now and start saving!

https://valeria-ray.gr8.com

Contents

Delicious Nepal Recipes

MMMMMMMMMMMMMMMMMMMMMMMMMMMMMMMMMMM

Chapter I - Nepalese Breakfasts

MMMMMMMMMMMMMMMMMMMMMMMMMMMMMMMMMM

(1) Spiced, Scrambled Eggs

This is Nepal's version of Western scrambled eggs. It includes butter, curry, cayenne pepper, onions and cumin, along with the fluffy eggs. It is often served on toast.

Serving Size: 6 Servings

Total Prep Time: ½ hour

List of Ingredients:

- 12 lightly beaten eggs, large
- ¼ cup of butter, softened
- 2 tablespoons of curry paste
- 2 pinches of cayenne pepper, ground
- 4 sliced red onions, small
- ¼ cup of clarified butter (ghee)
- 1 teaspoon of cumin, ground
- 1 teaspoon of coriander, ground
- ¼ cup + 2 tablespoons of chopped cilantro, fresh

MMMMMMMMMMMMMMMMMMMMMMMMMMMMMMMMMM

Methods:

1. Heat the ghee in skillet on med. heat. Fry onions, cayenne pepper, coriander and cumin till onions become soft. Add curry paste and stir in. Set aside.
2. In another skillet, melt butter on med-low heat. Pour in eggs. Stir while cooking till eggs set. Mix in onion mixture. Serve with cilantro as garnish.

(2) Millet-Buckwheat Pancakes

Using millet flour gives these pancakes a crumbly texture, while buckwheat makes the texture softer. When you mix the two grains, you get these nutritious, delicious pancakes that make a great breakfast option.

Serving Size: 4-5 Servings

Total Prep Time: 40 minutes

List of Ingredients:

- ½ teaspoons of baking powder
- 1 teaspoon of sugar, granulated
- 1 tablespoon of flax seed, ground
- 1 or 2 eggs, large
- Butter, to grease pan
- 1 cup of milk, whole
- ½ cup of flour, millet
- ½ cup of flour, buckwheat
- 1 pinch salt
- Berries, other fruits and honey, to top

MMMMMMMMMMMMMMMMMMMMMMMMMMMMMMMMM

Methods:

1. Add baking powder, sugar, pinch salt, flaxseed and both flours in large bowl. Mix well.
2. In separate bowl, whisk eggs and milk lightly. Add to the flour mixture.
3. Whisk mixtures together till there are no lumps and the batter is airy and light.
4. Allow batter to rest for about five minutes.
5. Place fry pan over med. heat. Lightly grease with butter.
6. Whisk batter and slowly pour into heated pan. This will need to be done in batches. Place lid on pan. Flip pancake when upper layer is firm. Cook on both sides.
7. Serve with fruits, berries and honey, as desired.

(3) Breakfasts in Nepal

This is a satisfying way to start your day. These potatoes are tasty and wonderful, and the accompanying brown sugar and garlic are suitably blended, making this dish an appealing choice for breakfast.

Serving Size: 4 Servings

Total Prep Time: 35 minutes

List of Ingredients:

- 1 tablespoon + 3 teaspoons of butter, softened
- 2 teaspoons of cumin, ground
- 2 teaspoons of coriander, ground
- 12 oz. of water, filtered
- 1 tablespoon of sugar, brown
- 8 oz. of pulped tomatoes
- 3 crushed cloves of garlic
- ½ teaspoons of turmeric
- 1 & 2/3 lbs. of cubed potatoes
- 1 handful of chopped coriander leaves

MMMMMMMMMMMMMMMMMMMMMMMMMMMMMMMMMM

Methods:

1. Boil potatoes and turmeric in large sized pot till tender. Drain. Set aside.

2. Heat butter in large sized pan. Fry garlic for two minutes.

3. Add water, pulped tomatoes and sugar and bring to boil. Reduce heat and gently simmer till mixture is reduced.

4. Add drained potatoes, coriander and cumin. Combine well. Gently simmer for about five minutes.

5. Season the mixture. Pile it onto individual plates. Garnish using coriander leaves. Serve.

(4) Round Bread – Gwaramari

Round bread translates literally into Nepalese as Gwaramari, in the Katmandu Valley region. It is often served with milk tea or chutney, and it is said to be best when it is served warm.

Serving Size: 4 Servings

Total Prep Time: 40 minutes + 1 hour or overnight setting time

List of Ingredients:

- 1 cup of water, filtered
- 12 cups of flour, all-purpose
- Oil, to fry
- 1 teaspoon each of turmeric powder, salt, sugar and baking powder

MMMMMMMMMMMMMMMMMMMMMMMMMMMMMMMMMMM

Methods:

1. Mix dry ingredients in medium bowl.
2. Slowly add water. Continue to mix till it has become a paste. It shouldn't be too runny.
3. Cover with cling wrap. Set aside for one hour or overnight.
4. Heat fry pan on med-high. Add ½" of oil for dipping.
5. Drop 1 tablespoon of batter into oil in pan.
6. Cook for about two minutes each side.
7. Place on paper towels to drain oil away. Serve when all are done.

(5) Chatamari Breakfast

This breakfast favorite is also served as a popular street food, and commonly called Nepali pizza. The toppings can be breakfast-centered or include tomatoes, minced meats and onions when served as street food.

Serving Size: 6 Servings

Total Prep Time: 1 hour

List of Ingredients:

For the rice base

- 1 cup of butter, unsalted
- 1 cup of water, filtered
- 3 beaten eggs, large
- 2 cups of flour, rice
- Salt, as desired

For the topping

- 3 tablespoons of butter
- 1 teaspoon of minced ginger
- 1 teaspoon of minced garlic
- ½ cup of tomatoes, diced
- ½ cup of onions, chopped finely
- ½ pound of chicken, minced or chopped
- Salt, as desired
- ½ teaspoons of black pepper, ground

MMMMMMMMMMMMMMMMMMMMMMMMMMMMMMMMM

Methods:

1. Heat the butter.
2. Fry the ginger, onions and garlic till light brown in color. Add salt, pepper and minced meat.
3. Add tomatoes right before the meat has finished cooking.
4. Cook till meat is almost done. Set aside.
5. Mix pinch of salt, along with water, eggs and flour, to make the batter.
6. Heat butter over pan.
7. Pour in batter. Spread into thin crust.
8. Cover pan. Cook on one side only for several minutes.
9. Don't flip the batter cake.
10. Place meat topping on cake. Cover. Cook for several more minutes. Serve hot.

Chapter II - Nepalese Dinners, Lunches, Sides and Appetizers

MMMMMMMMMMMMMMMMMMMMMMMMMMMMMMMMMM

(6) Nepalese Chicken Curry

This dish has a flavor that's different from the countries around it. If you like spicy Asian meals, you will note the differing spice amounts that are used in this recipe. They give it a unique taste that many people love. See if you do, too.

Serving Size: 4 Servings

Total Prep Time: 1 & ½ hour + 2+ hours marinating time

List of Ingredients:

- 4 chopped tomatoes, medium
- 8 & ½ fl. oz. of chicken stock
- 2 sliced onions
- 2 tablespoons of oil, vegetable
- 1 & ½ lbs. of chicken drumsticks and thighs
- 5 & 1/3 oz. of yogurt, natural
- 2 chopped cloves of garlic
- 1/3 oz. of peeled, chopped ginger
- ½ teaspoons of fennel seeds
- 5 cardamom pods, green
- 4 cloves
- 2 teaspoons of cumin seeds
- 1 teaspoon of turmeric
- 1 stick of cinnamon
- ¼ teaspoons of chili powder
- ½ teaspoons of mace
- 2 bay leaves

MMMMMMMMMMMMMMMMMMMMMMMMMMMMMMMM

Methods:

1. Crush cardamom pods. Remove seeds.
2. Place small fry pan on med. heat. Add fennel seeds and cardamom seeds.
3. Heat the seeds while you stir frequently till fragrant. Allow to cool a bit. Add to mortar and pestle with garlic and ginger. Grind till they form a paste.
4. Add yogurt to large sized bowl with pinch of kosher salt and spice paste. Combine by stirring.
5. Add chicken. Stir till covered completely. Cover. Leave in the refrigerator and marinate for two hours or more.
6. Preheat oven to 350F. Heat oil on med-high in large, oven-proof, deep pan. Remove chicken from marinade. Reserve marinade. Add chicken to pan.
7. Fry chicken for six minutes till first side browns well. Turn them over and cook for three more minutes. Use tongs to remove chicken from pan. Transfer to plate. Set aside.
8. While pan still holds heat, add cinnamon, cloves, cumin seeds and onions. Reduce heat to low. Sauté spices and onions till onions turn golden brown.

9. Add chili powder, turmeric and mace. Cook for another minute. Add stock to pan. Simmer for several minutes.

10. Add leftover yogurt and tomatoes to pan. Add bay leaves and stir till they combine. Nestle chicken on the top. Pour juices over the mixture.

11. Transfer mixture, uncovered, to oven. Bake for 40 to 45 minutes till meat has cooked through. Remove from oven. Serve promptly.

(7) Almond Honey Chicken

This Nepalese honey chicken includes honey, raisins, cream and yogurt. It has a subtle sweetness that works well with succulent chicken, giving you a delightful taste.

Serving Size: 2-4 Servings

Total Prep Time: 45 minutes + 4 hours marinating time

List of Ingredients:

- 1 & ¾ oz. of chopped almonds
- 2 tablespoons of honey, pure
- 1 & ¾ oz. of raisins
- ½ cup of cream
- ½ cup of yogurt
- 1 & 1/10 lb. of breast fillet, chicken
- ½ teaspoons of turmeric
- ½ teaspoons of cumin seeds
- ½ lemon, rind and juice

MMMMMMMMMMMMMMMMMMMMMMMMMMMMMMMMMMM

Methods:

1. Stir cream, yogurt, turmeric, cumin seeds, lemon rind and juice, honey, raisins and almonds together. Blend well. Place in bag with chicken and marinate for four hours.

2. Place marinated chicken in baking dish and spoon remainder of marinade on top of it.

3. Bake in oven for 35 minutes at 350F. Remove and serve.

(8) Chicken Mango Tartari

Do you have some mango at home that needs to be used? This is a great recipe to try it with. You can add more chili paste if you like HEAT in your dishes. If you prepare it with an immersion blender, it will make for an easier cleanup.

Serving Size: 2-4 Servings

Total Prep Time: 1 hour & 10 minutes

List of Ingredients:

- 4 tablespoons of clarified butter (ghee)
- 1 teaspoon of peppercorns, black
- 1 tablespoon of chili paste
- 1 tablespoon of minced ginger root
- 1 tablespoon of minced garlic
- 1 cup of diced onion
- ½ teaspoons of turmeric
- 1 teaspoon of cumin powder
- 2 cups of diced mangoes, ripe
- 2 pounds of sliced chicken breast meat
- Kosher salt
- Ground pepper
- 1 tablespoon of lemon juice
- For garnish: 1 tablespoon of fresh, chopped cilantro

MMMMMMMMMMMMMMMMMMMMMMMMMMMMMMMMMMMM

Methods:

1. Heat 2 tablespoons of butter in non-stick sauté pan.
2. Fry peppercorns for ½ minute.
3. Add onion and turmeric. Sauté till they are translucent
4. Add cumin powder, garlic and ginger. Stir well for about a minute.
5. Place chunks of mango into onion mixture. Combine. Sauté for about five minutes, allowing the mango to sweat.
6. Add salt, pepper and chili paste. Stir well and incorporate all ingredients.
7. Simmer mango mixture for about 10 more minutes. Reduce mixture by ½.
8. Remove from the heat. Transfer to food processor and puree mixture into mango sauce.
9. Season pieces of chicken with salt, pepper and lemon juice in large sized bowl.
10. Heat 2 tablespoons butter in non-stick pan. Add chicken mixture. Brown on med. heat for eight to 10 minutes. Chicken should almost be done.
11. Add pureed mango sauce to chicken. Combine well and coat all chicken pieces.

12. Lower heat. Allow meat to braise for 12-15 minutes, till chicken is tender and curry is thicker.

13. Adjust seasoning, as desired.

14. Garnish with cilantro. Serve.

(9) Bamboo Shoots & Beans

This Nepali dish is very popular, and the bamboo sourness is an integral part. The dish also includes black eyed peas, making it a hearty meal for your family or guests.

Serving Size: 3 Servings

Total Prep Time: 1 hour & 10 minutes

List of Ingredients:

- 6 tablespoons of oil, cooking
- 2 cups of tomatoes, chopped
- 1 cup of broth, chicken
- ½ teaspoons of turmeric
- 2 cups of peeled, cubed potatoes
- 1 cup of bamboo shoots, fermented
- 3 red chilies, dried
- 1 cup of chopped onion
- 1 cup of overnight-soaked black-eyed peas
- 1 tablespoon of mustard paste, whole
- 1 teaspoon of minced ginger
- 1 teaspoon of minced garlic
- 1 tablespoon of curry powder
- 1 teaspoon of chili powder
- Kosher salt & ground black pepper
- For garnishing: 1 tablespoon of cilantro, chopped

MMMMMMMMMMMMMMMMMMMMMMMMMMMMMMMMMM

Methods:

1. Heat 3 tablespoons oil in fry pan. Fry the bamboo shoots till light brown. Set aside.
2. Fry the dried chilies till they turn dark. Add onions. Sauté till light brown.
3. Add salt, pepper, mustard paste, garlic, ginger, chili powder and curry powder. Fry for a minute or so on low heat.
4. Add the potatoes to onion mixture. Sauté for four to five minutes over med. heat.
5. Add broth, tomatoes, bamboo shoots and soaked beans to potato mixture. Stir and combine well.
6. Bring to boil. Allow to simmer for 17-20 minutes on low heat till the potatoes are tender and gravy is at your desired consistency.
7. Garnish with cilantro and serve.

(10) Samsa - Samosa

This appetizer is well-known in Nepal, and in neighboring India, as well. In this recipe it's made from spinach and eggs, in pastries that are deep-fried till they are crispy. It's simple, but delicious.

Serving Size: 2-3 Servings

Total Prep Time: 1 & ½ hours

List of Ingredients:

- 1 onion
- 17 & 2/3 oz. of spinach
- 1 large egg
- 7 oz. of flour, all-purpose
- Coriander, fresh

MMMMMMMMMMMMMMMMMMMMMMMMMMMMMMMMM

Methods:

1. Combine ½ cup water, egg and flour to create dough. Set aside for ½ hour.
2. To make the filling, chop onions. Fry them for five minutes. Chop spinach and add to the onions. Fry for five more minutes. Cut coriander. Add to mixture, with salt & pepper.
3. Cut dough into 10 pieces. Roll all pieces into small circles. Place spoonful of filling in middle of the circles. Close their edges and form triangles. Bake at 390F for ½ hour.
4. Remove from oven and serve.

(11) Vegetable Pakora

Pakora is another street food quite popular in Nepal. It is sometimes compared to Japanese tempura. This vegetable version is the most common, and is typically served with tomato chutney.

Serving Size: 8-10 Servings

Total Prep Time: ½ hour

List of Ingredients:

- 2 halved tomatoes, ripe, large
- 7 oz. of flour, chickpea
- 2 chopped green chilies, long
- 1 & ¾ oz. of leaves, baby spinach
- 3 & ½ oz. of grated potatoes
- 1 thinly sliced onion
- 3 & ½ oz. of thin-sliced cabbage
- 34 oz. of oil, to deep fry
- 2 teaspoons of garam masala (spice mix)
- 2 teaspoons of coriander, ground
- 2 teaspoons of cumin, ground
- Kosher salt, as desired

To serve:

- Tomato chutney
- Coriander, chopped
- 1 pinch ground cumin
- 1 pinch ground coriander
- chili flakes and salt, to taste

MMMMMMMMMMMMMMMMMMMMMMMMMMMMMMMMMM

Methods:

1. For tomato chutney, preheat the oven to 325F.

2. Place tomatoes on cookie sheet lined with baking paper. Roast for 50 minutes to one hour, till they are deep red in color and very tender.

3. Remove tomato skins. Place in food processor with chili salt & flakes, coriander and cumin. Blend till texture is smooth.

4. Heat oil in large pan. Place salt, garam masala, coriander, cumin, green chili, spinach, potato, cabbage and onion in large sized bowl. Mix well.

5. Sprinkle chick pea flour. Mix well. Slowly add 5 fl. oz. of water. Continue to mix till veggies are sticking to each other.

6. Place 1 tablespoon-size pieces of the mixture gently into hot oil. Fry in batches for three to four minutes each. Gently turn till golden.

7. Remove pakora with slotted spoon. Place on paper towels to absorb extra oil. Serve hot, along with tomato chutney and coriander.

(12) Nepalese Lentil Soup

This recipe looks so simple (and it is), so the taste will be beyond your expectations. There is a wonderful ingredient combination, and the spices complement one another quite well.

Serving Size: 6 Servings

Total Prep Time: 1 hour

List of Ingredients:

- 3 cups of canned tomatoes, undrained
- 1 diced potato
- 1 peeled, diced carrot
- 1 chili pepper, fresh
- 2 minced garlic cloves
- 1 & ½ cup of chopped onions
- 1 tablespoon of oil, vegetable
- 6 cups of water, filtered
- 1 & ½ cup of rinsed, dried lentils
- 2 teaspoons of cumin
- 1 & ½ teaspoons of salt, kosher
- 1 tablespoon of chopped cilantro, fresh
- 2 teaspoons of coriander, ground

MMMMMMMMMMMMMMMMMMMMMMMMMMMMMMMM

Methods:

1. Bring water and lentils to boil. Reduce heat and cover. Simmer till tender.

2. Heat the oil. Sauté chili, onions and garlic for about five minutes.

3. Add cumin, coriander, potatoes and carrots. Sauté for a minute, and stir to keep them from sticking.

4. Remove pan from heat. Set aside.

5. When lentils become tender, chop tomatoes and stir into pot.

6. Add sautéed veggies, cilantro and salt. Cover. Simmer for 12-15 minutes. All the vegetables should be tender. Plate and serve.

(13) Alu Chop – Potato Rolls

The addition of potatoes to this recipe creates a wonderfully light texture. You can bake the rolls up to three or four weeks ahead of time. They can be frozen in foil and thawed, to enjoy. **Serving Size: 3 Servings**

Total Prep Time: 50 minutes + 3 hours chilling time

List of Ingredients:

- A loaf de-crusted, sliced bread, white
- ½ teaspoons of turmeric powder
- 2 chopped chili peppers
- 1 piece of finely chopped ginger root
- 2 chopped garlic cloves
- 7 oz. of peas, green
- 1 chopped onion
- 2 cubed tomatoes
- 3 peeled, cubed potatoes

MMMMMMMMMMMMMMMMMMMMMMMMMMMMMMMMM

Methods:

1. Fry chilies, onions and garlic for five minutes. Add potatoes. Fry for three more minutes.
2. Add ginger, turmeric, peas and tomatoes plus ½ cup water. Simmer for 15 minutes.
3. Dip bread slices quickly in water. Press out surplus water.
4. Distribute 1 & ½ tablespoons of potato mixture over bread. Roll up. Repeat with remaining slices. Place in refrigerator for several hours.
5. Fry rolls in the hot oil till they turn a golden brown. Serve.

(14) Nepalese Basmati Rice

This rice side is easy to prepare but it has wonderfully complex flavors. The dish has a salty and sweet element, and the spices work so well off each other, you'll enjoy it a lot.

Serving Size: 6 Servings

Total Prep Time: 1 hour & 10 minutes

List of Ingredients:

- 2 sticks of cinnamon
- 1 peeled, chopped onion, medium
- 2 tablespoons of veg. oil
- 1 & ½ cups of basmati rice, uncooked
- 1 bay leaf
- 2 cloves, whole
- 2 oz. of raisins, golden
- 4 oz. of cashews, whole or halved
- 1 teaspoon of salt, kosher

MMMMMMMMMMMMMMMMMMMMMMMMMMMMMMMMMM

Methods:

1. Wash rice a few times. Allow to soak for ½ hour. Drain well.

2. Heat oil in skillet on med-low. Cook the onion till it's soft.

3. Add all spices and ingredients except for salt to large pan. Stir fry for two minutes on med. heat.

4. Add 2 cups water and salt to pan. Bring to boil. Cover. Reduce heat to low.

5. Simmer mixture for 15 to 20 minutes. Add extra water if you need to. Rice should be fluffy and tender, and all water should be absorbed.

6. Remove cinnamon sticks, bay leaf and cloves. Serve.

(15) Nepalese Chicken

This is a mother's version of a classic dish in Nepal. It is served either as lunch or dinner, and is sometimes served with gravy.

Serving Size: 2-4 Servings

Total Prep Time: 55 minutes + 30 minutes refrigerator time

List of Ingredients:

- 3 tablespoons of oil for cooking
- 3 chopped cloves of garlic
- 1 teaspoon of ginger root, chopped
- 4 tablespoons of yogurt
- 2 tomatoes
- 2 capsicums, red
- 1 onion
- 2 & ¼ lbs. of cubed chicken fillet
- 1 teaspoon of pepper, black
- ½ teaspoons of cumin seed
- 1 teaspoon of powdered coriander
- 1 teaspoon salt, kosher

MMMMMMMMMMMMMMMMMMMMMMMMMMMMMMMM

Methods:

1. Marinate chicken by mixing cubes with 1 tablespoon of yogurt, 1 teaspoon of garlic and salt and ground pepper. Place mixture in refrigerator for ½ hour.

2. Chop 1 tomato, onions and capsicums into cubes. Pour 1 tablespoon oil in lidded pan. Fry veggies over low heat for ½ hour.

3. Add pinch of ground pepper. Cover pan. Allow to heat while you perform next steps.

4. Place marinated chicken in pan and fry till golden brown. Drain. Set it aside.

5. In a separate pan, heat tablespoons of oil and fry 1 de-seeded, peeled, lightly crushed tomato.

6. After a minute, add chopped garlic, cumin seeds and 1 teaspoon of coriander powder. Fry mixture for five minutes or more.

7. Add 3 tablespoons of the yogurt. If you prefer more gravy, use more yogurt. Add fried chicken to yogurt mixture.

8. Allow to cook till gravy has thickened.

9. Add this mixture to onion and capsicum mixture in other pan over low heat. You do not have to mix them. Serve with white rice.

(16) Spicy Nepali Potato Salad

It's not surprising that this is a common Nepali dish. It's SO tasty! Most people have had this dish at least once in their lives. It's an inexpensive, fresh recipe, too.

Serving Size: 5 Servings

Total Prep Time: 35 minutes

List of Ingredients:

- 1 chopped green chili, long
- 1 & ¾ green peas, blanched, refreshed with cold water
- 1 & 1/10 pound of potatoes, small
- 2 tablespoons of oil, vegetable
- 2 teaspoons of sesame seeds, black
- ¼ cup of lemon juice, fresh
- 1 teaspoon of fenugreek seeds
- 1 teaspoon of turmeric, ground
- To serve: fresh leaves of coriander

MMMMMMMMMMMMMMMMMMMMMMMMMMMMMMMMM

Methods:

1. Places potatoes in sauce pan. Cover with lightly salted water. Gently simmer till cooked through. Set aside till cooled enough that you can handle them. Peel and cube.

2. Mix peas with potatoes, along with sesame seeds, chilies and lemon juice. Set the dish aside.

3. Pour the oil into small sized fry pan on med. heat. When oil becomes hot, add fenugreek seeds and turmeric powder. Once fenugreek seeds have turned somewhat brown, pour oil and other pan ingredients into bowl with the potatoes. Mix well.

4. Use fresh coriander to garnish. Serve.

(17) Mutton Momo

These lamb dumplings are steamed or fried, and may be served with broth or dipping sauce. The addition of coriander and ginger gives them a taste that makes them unique when compared to other dumplings.

Serving Size: 25 Servings

Total Prep Time: 1 & ½ hours

List of Ingredients:

- 2 tablespoons of clarified butter (ghee)
- 1 & 1/3 cups of flour, plain + more for dusting
- Tomato achar, sliced red chilies & spring onions for serving
- For the lamb filling
- 1 chopped bird's eye chili, red
- 2 crushed cloves of garlic
- ½ chopped onion
- 8 oz. of lamb, minced
- 1 small grated piece of ginger
- 2 tablespoons of chopped coriander leaves
- 5 peppercorns
- ¼ teaspoons of black pepper, ground
- 1 teaspoon of coriander, ground
- 1 teaspoon of cumin, ground
- ½ teaspoons of turmeric, ground

MMMMMMMMMMMMMMMMMMMMMMMMMMMMMMMMMM

Methods:

1. To create the momo wrappers, combine the flour and ¼ teaspoons of salt in large sized bowl. Make a deep well in middle, add clarified butter and 4 & ¼ fl. oz. of hot water. Mix till it forms dough.

2. Place on lightly floured cutting board. Knead for about five minutes, till it is smooth.

3. Place the dough in pre-greased bowl. Cover with cling wrap. Set in warm place to rest for ½ hour.

4. To create filling, combine all lamb filling ingredients in medium bowl. Cover with cling wrap. Place in refrigerator until you need it.

5. Roll dough out onto lightly floured cutting board until it is only about ½ inch in thickness.

6. Use round cookie cutter to make 25 rounds. Place a teaspoons of lamb filling in middle of all rounds. Brush edges with a bit of water.

7. Bring edges up from three points of rounds. Press edges in, forming dumplings shaped like pyramids.

8. Line large sized steamer basket. Set over large pot of water at a simmer.

9. Steam the momo, several at a time, for seven to nine minutes. They should be cooked through and tender.

10. Scatter the momo with onions and chilies. Serve.

(18) Nepalese Veggie Pulao

This is an easy dish that is SO packed with wonderful flavors. The whole spices make it a fragrant dish, and the ingredients make it light on your stomach, so it won't over-fill you.

Serving Size: 4 Servings

Total Prep Time: 55 minutes

List of Ingredients:

- 1/3 teaspoons of cumin seeds
- ½ cup of green peas
- 1 & ¼ cups of rice, basmati
- 1 bay leaf
- ½ teaspoons turmeric, as desired
- 2 cardamom pods, black
- 6 cloves, whole
- ½ teaspoons of minced ginger
- ¼ teaspoons of cinnamon
- 3 halved chilies, green
- 1 teaspoon of minced garlic
- ½ chopped tomato, large
- 1 chopped onion, yellow, large
- Salt, as desired
- 1 tablespoon of lemon juice, fresh

MMMMMMMMMMMMMMMMMMMMMMMMMMMMMMM

Methods:

1. Rinse the rice well. Soak in water for 45 minutes or so.

2. Heat 2 tablespoons oil in pan. Add the cumin seeds. Allow them to become hotter until they start changing color. Add cinnamon, cardamom pods, bay leaf and turmeric.

3. Add chilies, ginger and garlic. Cook over med. heat for barely one minute.

4. Add peas, onion and tomato. Cook for three minutes.

5. Drain water from the rice. Add to pan. Stir gently for about one minute and combine well.

6. Add 2 & ½ cups water. Salt as desired.

7. Cook over high heat. Stir gently and continuously.

8. When water has been almost fully absorbed, add the lemon juice.

9. Lower heat. Cover pan. Allow to cook for about seven minutes more. Rice should be cooked completely. Serve promptly.

(19) Palak Paneer

This dish is a true crowd-pleaser. If you are trying to show off your Nepali cooking style, this dish will do it. It features paneer cubes soaked in a spinach gravy, so tasty!

Serving Size: 2 Servings

Total Prep Time: 20 minutes

List of Ingredients:

- ¼ cup of cream
- 1 grated piece of ginger root
- 2 chopped chilies
- 7 oz. of cubed paneer
- 2 chopped onions
- 2 chopped tomatoes
- 2 & ¼ lbs. of chopped spinach

MMMMMMMMMMMMMMMMMMMMMMMMMMMMMMMMMM

Methods:

1. Stir fry spinach for five minutes. Place in food processor and puree.
2. Fry chili and onion for several minutes.
3. Add remaining ingredients. Heat mixture for about five minutes, till everything is heated through. Serve hot.

(20) Phulko Tarkari - Egg Curry

In this recipe, various ingredients will surround the rice. You can make this dish with just veggies, but this version is made with eggs. The recipe is easy to make, and the result is delicious.

Serving Size: 3-4 Servings

Total Prep Time: 50 minutes

List of Ingredients:

- 1 grated piece ginger root
- 2 chopped garlic cloves
- 1 chopped onion
- 3 cut tomatoes
- 3 peeled, diced potatoes
- 6 boiled eggs, large
- Handful of cut coriander
- ½ teaspoons of turmeric

MMMMMMMMMMMMMMMMMMMMMMMMMMMMMMMMMMM

Methods:

1. Fry eggs for several minutes in hot oil. Slice in half.
2. Fry garlic and onion for several minutes. Add potatoes. Stir-fry for a couple minutes.
3. Add salt, pepper, ½ cup water, turmeric and ginger root. Simmer for 12-15 minutes.
4. Stir in tomato. Heat for another minute.
5. Place eggs on plate. Arrange with curry. Sprinkle using coriander. Serve.

(21) Nepalese Peas & Potato Curry

This curry has a rich flavor, and it's fairly easy to make. It's inexpensive, and you can put it together quickly, without advance notice of arriving guests.

Serving Size: 3-4 Servings

Total Prep Time: 50 minutes

List of Ingredients:

- 1 cup of filtered water, hot
- 1 teaspoon of cumin, ground
- 1 or 2 green chilies, mild
- 1 sliced onion, large
- 1 tablespoon of oil to cook
- 1 teaspoon of grated ginger root
- 2 teaspoons of chopped garlic
- 2 teaspoons of coriander, ground
- 1 chopped tomato, large
- 2 cups of peas
- 2 cups of peeled, cubed potatoes
- 1 teaspoon of salt, kosher
- ½ teaspoons of turmeric, ground
- ½ teaspoons of pepper, black, ground

MMMMMMMMMMMMMMMMMMMMMMMMMMMMMMMMM

Methods:

1. Heat the oil in sauce pan. Fry the onion till golden and soft. Stir in salt, turmeric, ginger, garlic, chili and pepper.
2. Continue to cook for two or three minutes. Add potatoes and stir.
3. Add the rest of the ingredients and the hot water.
4. Simmer till the veggies have cooked. Thicken as desired. Serve with rice.

(22) Lamb Sekuwa - Grilled Marinated Lamb

Grilled meat is another popular street food in Nepal. It is sometimes paired with achar (tomato pickle) or beaten rice. It is served in restaurants, too – but you'll love it especially after you've made it yourself!

Serving Size: 4 Servings

Total Prep Time: 35 minutes + overnight refrigeration/marinating

List of Ingredients:

For the marinade

- ½ cup of yogurt, plain
- 2 chopped chilies, small, green
- 1 tablespoon of lemon juice
- 1 teaspoon of salt, kosher
- 1 tablespoon of chopped garlic
- 1 tablespoon of chopped ginger
- 1 teaspoon of garam masala (mixed spices)
- ½ teaspoons of turmeric, ground

For the skewers

- 2 & ¼ lbs. of trimmed, boneless leg of lamb
- 1 teaspoon of lemon juice
- Salt, flaked
- 2 tablespoons of clarified butter (ghee)
- To serve, as desired:
- Tomato pickle
- Beaten rice

MMMMMMMMMMMMMMMMMMMMMMMMMMMMMMMMMM

Methods:

1. Combine ingredients for marinade in large mixing bowl. Add lamb meat. Combine well and coat lamb. Cover. Marinate overnight in refrigerator.

2. Preheat grill to med-high. Remove lamb from marinade. Thread onto skewers.

3. Grill for eight to 10 minutes. Turn frequently while basting with clarified butter, till lamb has browned on each side and has cooked fully through.

4. Remove skewers from the grill. Season as desired. Drizzle with the lemon juice.

5. Serve with tomato pickle, beaten rice and other condiments of choice.

(23) Aloo Masu Chop – Potato Croquettes and Spiced Beef

These Nepalese croquettes are wonderful snacks for parties. For this recipe, mashed potatoes are filled with beef and rolled in fresh bread crumbs, before being deep-fried to deliciousness.

Serving Size: 4 Servings

Total Prep Time: 1 hour & 10 minutes + 25 minutes of chilling time

List of Ingredients:

- 2 cups of breadcrumbs, fresh
- 2 beaten eggs, large
- 1/3 cup of flour, plain
- ¼ cup of water or beef stock
- 1 de-seeded, chopped green chili, long
- 6 & 1/3 oz. of beef mince
- 1 teaspoon of ginger, grated finely
- 2 chopped cloves of garlic
- 2 & 2/3 lbs. of sliced potatoes
- ½ chopped onion, brown
- 2 tablespoons of oil, vegetable, + extra for frying
- 1 pinch of Szechuan pepper powder
- Salt, kosher
- ½ teaspoons of black pepper
- For serving: lime pickle and green chutney

MMMMMMMMMMMMMMMMMMMMMMMMMMMMMMMMMMMM

Methods:

1. Bring large sized sauce pan of lightly salted water up to boil. Add potatoes. Cook for 12-15 minutes, till they are tender.

2. Drain the potatoes and return them to sauce pan. Place on low heat for a couple more minutes so excess water evaporates. Mash till smooth. Season as desired.

3. Heat veg. oil in large sauce pan on med. heat. Add onion. Cook for six to seven minutes till it softens. Add ginger and garlic. Cook for one to two more minutes, till they are aromatic.

4. Raise heat to high. Add Szechuan pepper, black pepper, chili and beef. Stir while cooking and break up any lumps, for four to five minutes, till mixture has browned evenly. Add stock. Stir and combine.

5. Lower heat. Cover pan. Simmer for 13-15 minutes. Remove lid. Cook for seven to eight more minutes till all liquid is absorbed. Stir regularly as cooking time nears its end. Remove from heat. Allow the mixture to cool.

6. Flatten ¼ cup of the mashed potatoes in your hand. Create a 3 & ½-inch circle.

7. Place 2 & ½ teaspoons of meat filling in middle. Wrap potato around filling. Form into egg shape. Set aside.

8. Repeat steps 6 and 7 with remaining potatoes and filling. Place balls in the refrigerator for about 15-20 minutes, till they are firm.

9. Place bread crumbs, flour and egg in three individual bowls. Roll balls in flour first. Dip them in the egg and then in bread crumbs.

10. Heat 4" of veg. oil in deep sauce pan. Deep fry your coquettes in small batches, each for four to five minutes. They should appear golden. Drain them on paper towels.

11. Serve with lime pickle and green chutney.

(24) Momo – Meat Dumplings

These meat-stuffed dumplings are among the most favorite dishes of Nepal. It is actually a prime example of the influence of Tibet on the cuisine of Nepal.

Serving Size: 4 Servings

Total Prep Time: 40 minutes

List of Ingredients:

- 1 grated ginger root piece
- 2 finely chopped garlic cloves
- 4 chopped green onions
- 14 oz. of pork, minced
- 12 wonton wrappers
- 1 tablespoon of chopped coriander
- ½ teaspoons of coriander seeds
- ½ teaspoons of curry powder

MMMMMMMMMMMMMMMMMMMMMMMMMMMMMMMMMMM

Methods:

1. Mix the coriander leaves and seeds, salt, ground pepper, curry powder, ginger root, garlic, onions and beef.
2. Divide this mixture into 12 balls. Place balls on wonton wrappers. Fold them. Seal edges well with water. Steam momo for 20 minutes. Remove and serve.

(25) Lemon Rice Freshness

is added to this dish by the presence of lemon. You'll like it because of its crunchiness, too. It makes a great summer rice salad.

Serving Size: 1-2 Servings

Total Prep Time: 2 hours & 55 minutes

List of Ingredients:

- 6 tablespoons of sugar, granulated
- 1 lemon
- 1 cup of cream
- 1 & ½ cup of milk, whole
- 3 & ½ oz. of rice

MMMMMMMMMMMMMMMMMMMMMMMMMMMMMMMMMM

Methods:

1. Heat up milk. Dissolve the sugar in hot milk. Grate lemon rind. Press out the juice.

2. Mix hot milk mixture with lemon zest, cream and rice. Place in baking dish. Place in 300F oven for 2 & ½ hours, stirring each ½ hour. If mixture seems thick, add a bit more milk.

3. After rice has cooked, stir in lemon juice and serve cold or hot.

Chapter III - Nepalese Desserts

MMMMMMMMMMMMMMMMMMMMMMMMMMMMMMMMMM

(26) Gajar Ko Halwa – Carrot Pudding

If you have a sweet tooth, this dish will take care of it for you. It is eaten as a dessert, and a snack, as well. It is made more often when carrots are most easily accessible in gardens.

Serving Size: 6-8 Servings

Total Prep Time: 40 minutes

List of Ingredients:

- ½ teaspoons of powdered cardamom
- 3 tablespoons of clarified butter
- 2 cups of sugar, granulated
- 1 cup of half & half
- 3 cups of milk, whole
- 2 pounds of carrots
- Almonds, chopped
- Saffron flakes

MMMMMMMMMMMMMMMMMMMMMMMMMMMMMMMMMMMM

Methods:

1. Grate the carrots. Place carrots, sugar, half & half and milk in sauce pan.
2. Boil till thick and then continuously stir.
3. Add saffron, cardamom and clarified butter. Stir over low heat till butter oozes from mixture.
4. Decorate with chopped almonds and serve them hot.

(27) Gulab Jamun

This spongy ball dessert is very traditional in the Middle East. It is especially wonderful when served with ice cream or fresh cream.

Serving Size: 12-14 Servings

Total Prep Time: 50 minutes

List of Ingredients:

- 1/8 cup of yogurt
- ½ stick of butter, unsalted
- Several drops of rose water
- 4 cardamom pods
- 1 & ½ cups of sugar, granulated
- 2 cups of water, filtered
- 2 cups of Carnation powder
- 1 cup of baking mix
- Oil to fry
- Milk

MMMMMMMMMMMMMMMMMMMMMMMMMMMMMMMM

Methods:

1. Heat the butter. Pour into large bowl. Add yogurt, carnation powder and baking mix. Blend them together.

2. Knead the mixture well. Add milk as needed. Make one smooth ball and allow it to rest for about ½ hour.

3. Make dough into 12 to 14 small-sized balls.

4. Heat water and add sugar. Bring to a boil, adding cardamom seeds. Allow to simmer. Boil and then simmer, till water is reduced by ½.

5. Heat oil till hot. Fry balls to golden brown.

6. Soak balls in syrup till they have doubled in size. Serve cold or hot.

(28) Burfi – Milk Cakes

Burfi is quite popular, not just in Nepal, but in India, as well.

It tastes somewhat like dough for sugar cookies. The sugar,

ghee and chick pea flour also give it a fudgy taste.

Serving Size: 2-4 Servings

Total Prep Time: 25 minutes

List of Ingredients:

- 1 cup of sugar, granulated
- ½ teaspoons of powdered cardamom
- ½ cup of clarified butter (ghee)
- 1 cup of cheese, ricotta

MMMMMMMMMMMMMMMMMMMMMMMMMMMMMMMMMM

Methods:

1. Mix the cardamom, cheese and sugar.
2. Fry mixture in clarified butter till it is golden brown in color.
3. Plate mixture and cut in diamond shapes.
4. Cool. Serve as a tasty dessert.

(29) Nepali Rice & Coconut Pudding

If you like milky desserts, you will love this dish. It has lots of raisins, coconuts and nuts. It may just be the best rice pudding you've ever had!

Serving Size: 4-6 Servings

Total Prep Time: 80 minutes

List of Ingredients:

- 3 & ½ oz. of shredded coconut, unsweetened
- 1 teaspoon of pepper, black
- ¾ cup of sugar, granulated
- 6 & ¾ pints of milk, whole
- 2 & ½ cups of rice
- 3 tablespoons of butter, unsalted
- Nuts and raisins, if you like

MMMMMMMMMMMMMMMMMMMMMMMMMMMMMMMMMMM

Methods:

1. Melt butter in large sauce pan. Add rice. Fry for five minutes.

2. Add nuts and coconut and fry for an additional five minutes.

3. Add milk gradually to mixture. After 3 pints of milk, cook for 8-10 minutes.

4. Add coconut. Add another 3 pints of milk. Cook for 30 minutes.

5. Add the sugar and black pepper.

6. Mixture should be creamy and thick by now. Add last of milk. Cook for 8 to 15 more minutes, till rice is cooked and quite thick. Add raisins, as desired, and serve.

(30) Rasgula – Syrupy Dessert

This is a popular, traditional Nepali dessert. It is often made for special occasions and festivals. It is among the most favored of all desserts in the Middle East and Asia.

Serving Size: 4-5 Servings

Total Prep Time: 1 hour & 45 minutes

List of Ingredients:

- 3 cups of water, filtered
- 1 & ½ cup of sugar, granulated
- 2 teaspoons of vinegar, white
- 34 fl. oz. of milk, homogenized

MMMMMMMMMMMMMMMMMMMMMMMMMMMMMMMMMM

Methods:

1. Bring milk to boil. Add vinegar. This will aid in separating the whey. Sift mixture onto muslin cloth and throw away liquid part.

2. Pour cold, filtered water over curd, cooling and washing it. Discard water. Hang cloth for 15-18 minutes, allowing excess water to drip completely off.

3. Place curd in food processor. Blend on high, creating a smooth consistency. If curd seems dry, you can add a teaspoons of water. Don't add too much water, though. Remove paste from food processor. Make into balls of one to two inches diameter.

4. Boil water in wide pan. Be sure you have two to three inches of water. Add the sugar to water, creating light syrup.

5. Continue to boil syrup. Drop curd balls gently into it. Cook balls for ½ hour to 45 minutes. Remove from heat. Allow to cool down.

6. Place the syrup and balls in container. Refrigerate but do not freeze. Serve it cold.

About the Author

A native of Indianapolis, Indiana, Valeria Ray found her passion for cooking while she was studying English Literature at Oakland City University. She decided to try a cooking course with her friends and the experience changed her forever. She enrolled at the Art Institute of Indiana which offered extensive courses in the culinary Arts. Once Ray dipped her toe in the cooking world, she never looked back.

When Valeria graduated, she worked in French restaurants in the Indianapolis area until she became the head chef at one of the 5-star establishments in the area. Valeria's attention to taste and visual detail caught the eye of a local business person who expressed an interest in publishing her recipes. Valeria began her secondary career authoring cookbooks and e-books which she tackled with as much talent and gusto as her first career. Her passion for food leaps off the page of her books which have colourful anecdotes and stunning pictures of dishes she has prepared herself.

Valeria Ray lives in Indianapolis with her husband of 15 years, Tom, her daughter, Isobel and their loveable Golden Retriever, Goldy. Valeria enjoys cooking special dishes in her large, comfortable kitchen where the family gets involved in preparing meals. This successful, dynamic chef is an inspiration to culinary students and novice cooks everywhere.

* * * * * * * * * * * * * * * * * * *

Author's Afterthoughts

Thank you for Purchasing my book and taking the time to read it from front to back. I am always grateful when a reader chooses my work and I hope you enjoyed it!

With the vast selection available online, I am touched that you chose to be purchasing my work and take valuable time out of your life to read it. My hope is that you feel you made the right decision.

I very much would like to know what you thought of the book. Please take the time to write an honest and informative review on Amazon.com. Your experience and opinions will be of great benefit to me and those readers looking to make an informed choice.

With much thanks,

Valeria Ray